j949.8   Stewart, Gail,
STE   1949-

        Romania.

$11.95

DATE			

ROMANIA

by
Gail B. Stewart

CRESTWOOD HOUSE
New York

Collier Macmillan Canada
Toronto

Maxwell Macmillan International Publishing Group
New York Oxford Singapore Sydney

Library of Congress Cataloging-in-Publication Data
Stewart, Gail, date.
    Romania / by Gail B. Stewart. — 1st ed.
        p.   cm. — (Places in the news)
    Includes index.
    Summary: Examines the historical and recent events that have kept Romania in the news, with an emphasis on the dictatorship of Ceausescu.
    ISBN 0-89686-600-9
    1. Romania—History—1944-   —Juvenile literature. [1. Romania—History.] I. Title. II. Series: Stewart, Gail. Places in the news.
DR267.S74   1991
949.8—dc20   90-24946
                                                                                                                   CIP
                                                                                                                   AC

Photo Credits
Photos courtesy of AP—Wide World Photos

CRESTWOOD HOUSE

Macmillan Publishing Company
866 Third Avenue
New York, NY 10022

Collier Macmillan Canada, Inc.
1200 Eglinton Avenue East
Suite 200
Don Mills, Ontario M3C 3N1

Produced by Flying Fish Studio

Printed in the United States of America

First Edition

10 9 8 7 6 5 4 3 2 1

CONTENTS

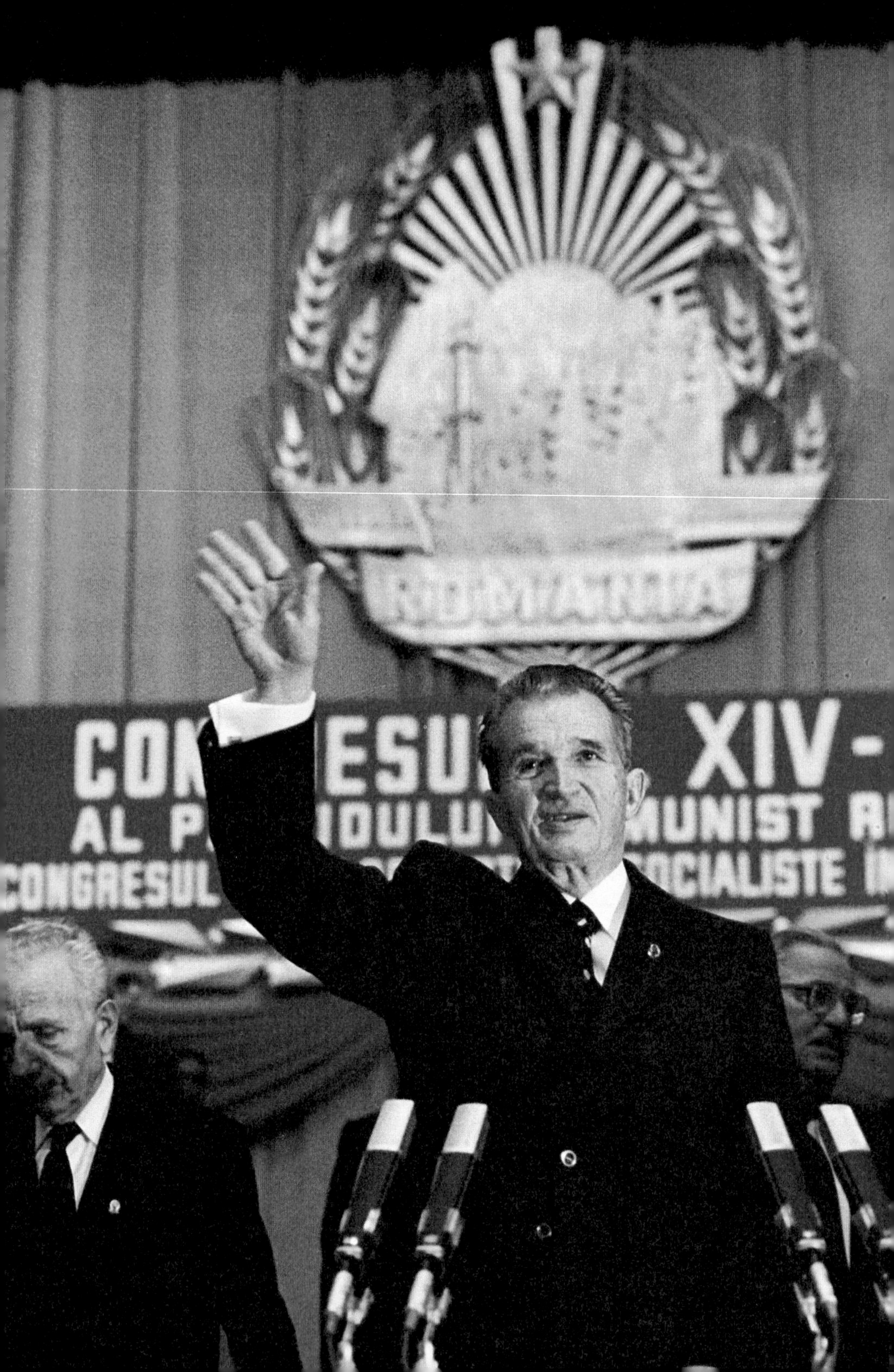
XIV-
MUNIST
OCIALISTE

ROMANIA IN THE NEWS

The president of Romania, Nicolae Ceausescu, cleared his throat before beginning to speak. The date was December 21, 1989. Ceausescu was about to make a speech to the people from the capitol in Bucharest. Romanian television was carrying the speech live, and tens of thousands were in the square watching in person.

Earlier in the week there had been trouble in the Romanian city of Timisoara. President Ceausescu (pronounced chow-CHES-ku) had ordered the army to shoot people who were demonstrating there. His speech on this day was important, for he wanted to prove that most of the people supported him. Trouble in one city did not mean that there was trouble anywhere else.

To project a strong, powerful image, the president's advisers had wanted to make sure Ceausescu looked fully in control on camera. They had hired hundreds of workers to stand near the speaker's platform and cheer. Some carried signs with CEAUSESCU IS THE HERO OF COMMUNIST ROMANIA written on them.

As the president began his speech, however, the unexpected happened. Jeers and boos came from the huge crowd. Shouts of "Ceausescu is a rat" and "Murderer, liar" drowned out Ceausescu's speech. This had never happened to Nicolae Ceausescu in his 24-year reign as president of Romania.

Nicolae Ceausescu, the former dictator of Romania, giving a speech 5
shortly before he and his wife, Elena, were arrested and executed in
December 1989

Witnesses said later that Ceausescu looked shocked. He was speechless. Immediately one of his advisers gave the word to the television cameramen to pull the plugs. In homes across the country television screens suddenly went black.

A Mob Scene in Bucharest

Realizing he could not go on with his speech, Ceausescu quickly retreated into his palace. Soon after, he gave orders to his security forces. They were told to fire on the crowds that were booing him.

Within moments the army began attacking the people. Machine-gun fire could be heard in the Bucharest city square. Tanks and other military vehicles rumbled into the area. Scores died and hundreds were wounded.

The President Flees

By the next morning the city square was littered with bodies of civilians. Even so, more and more Romanians were gathering to shout insults at the president outside his palace walls. Ceausescu's secret police, the Securitate, continued to fire at the protesters. However, many soldiers of the Romanian army refused to shoot civilians. Instead, they sided with the protesters, trading bullets and insults with the Securitate.

Elsewhere there were other signs of the Romanian people's revolt against President Ceausescu. The govern-

6   *A group of young Romanians celebrate on Christmas Day 1989 after Romanian television announced the arrest of Nicolae and Elena Ceausescu.*

ment-owned television station was taken over by rebels, who renamed the station Free Romanian Television. Television bulletins informed viewers that the government was being overthrown. The new government, according to the announcements, was called the National Salvation Front, or NSF.

Ceausescu realized that he could count on neither the army nor the people for support. His Securitate forces, strong as they were, could not hold off the mobs of people forever. Ceausescu and his wife, Elena, herself a key part of the government, escaped in the white presidential helicopter. Within hours the president's luxurious palace was in flames.

Surrounded

Ceausescu and his wife were heading for a military base in Boteni, a town just north of Bucharest, from which they hoped to flee Romania. However, when the helicopter touched down in Boteni, angry peasants surrounded it. They refused to move, blocking the helicopter until army troops came.

President Ceausescu and his wife were arrested by the army. They were charged with grave crimes—including mass murder, abuse of power and "destroying Romania." Ceausescu, according to witnesses, refused to answer during his hasty trial. He angrily shouted that he was the president and that they had no right to treat him in such a manner. Free Romanian Television broadcast portions of the trial. Viewers watched as Ceausescu and his wife, clothed in expensive fur overcoats, sat behind two small tables.

300 Volunteers

The military trial took less than two hours. Both Nicolae and Elena Ceausescu were found guilty of the stated crimes. Justice was swift. They were immediately brought before a firing squad.

There was no shortage of volunteers for the three-person firing squad. Some 300 soldiers offered their services.

Nicolae and Elena Ceausescu were executed just before dark on Christmas Day 1989. They wore no blindfolds. Over and over Free Romanian Television showed closeup shots of the dead president lying on the ground, his eyes open and his face colorless.

"He Was the Devil"

Nicolae Ceausescu was called the president of Romania. However, the office of president in Romania was very different from its counterpart in the United States. Ceausescu was a dictator, a person who holds total control of a country. He was the only one who decided the laws Romanians lived by. Only he controlled the economy, the military and the politics of his country.

At the time of his arrest, no one in Romania supported Ceausescu—except the Securitate.

Doina Gyorky, a Romanian farmer, said, "I won't even say the man's name aloud—nor will anyone I know. It is a hated name, and I feel as if I should spit after I say it. He was a murderer, who cared nothing for Romania. He was the devil; he is dead and I am glad."

Under Nicolae Ceausescu's rule Romania became one of the most horrible places on earth in which to live. Ceausescu maintained an iron grip on Romania, and he kept the condition of the country hidden from the rest of the world. No reporters, whether from radio, television or newspapers, had been able to describe what Romanians were forced to endure. Only now, since Ceausescu's death, are some of the unbelievable details being told.

The World Is Watching

Romania is in the news today for several reasons. For one, the people there are deciding on a new style of government. They are eager to erase all signs of the dictator who turned their country into a disaster. In May 1990 the Romanian people went to the polls to vote. It was the first time in 45 years that an election had not been controlled by the Communist party.

Another reason that the world is watching Romania is that the country has many problems to solve, a great many of them caused by Ceausescu and his greed for money and power. Because of him, there are matters of life and death that need to be addressed—and quickly.

Citizens in Bucharest look happily at a broken image of Ceausescu after it was thrown out of a public building. The dictator controlled Romania for 24 years.

In the coming years Romania will be in the process of rebuilding. The economy is in a shambles. People have nothing to eat. The air is black and dirty. Medical care is almost nonexistent.

"Ours is a country on the brink of hell," says a teacher from Bucharest. "In other countries people talk about their futures, what tomorrow will bring. Here it is much different. In Romania we wonder if we even have a tomorrow."

ROMANIA BEFORE CEAUSESCU

Nicolae Ceausescu was a dictator in a land that has long been used to dictators. Through the centuries Romanians have been conquered by many different peoples, who demanded total control over their country.

Changing Boundaries

Even in ancient times Romania seemed always on the verge of being seized by a new king. Part of the reason is the country's geography. Romania is located on the Black Sea, on what is called the Balkan Peninsula. The country has more than 150 miles of prime coastline—a great asset for trade and defense. And because the large Danube River flows through

POLAND

SOVIET UNION

CZECHOSLOVAKIA

HUNGARY

R O M A N I A

• Timisoara

• Bucharest

YUGOSLAVIA

Black

Sea

BULGARIA

13

Farming has been a way of life in Romania since ancient times. Because the Danube River flows through the country, the soil is very rich and it is easy to grow crops and raise livestock.

Romania, the country's soil is excellent for growing almost anything.

Romania has been invaded and controlled by many powers. Long ago, in the second century, the Romans conquered it and merged with the native tribes. The name *Romania* means "land of the Romans." The country later was overrun by the Huns, the Slavs and the Turks. The Russians also controlled Romania for a time.

Each time Romania changed hands, the boundaries changed a little too. The country is made up of separate districts, or states. Romania has consisted of anywhere from two to seven such states—with names like Moldavia and Transylvania.

Over the centuries various kings and dictators added new territory to Romania, land that they had seized from nearby countries. During this time the basic way of life for Romanians did not change much. Wealthy landowners used peasants to work large farms. The wealthy had political "muscle." In other words, they were able to gain favors from the government, which helped them keep their wealth. The peasants, on the other hand, were not represented at all. This system did not change, no matter what king or dictator was in power.

Communism Comes to Romania

In the years leading up to World War II, Romania was dominated by extreme right-wing conservatives. These were people who did not want any reforms at all. Many people in the country supported the Fascist policies of the Iron Guard and the League of National Christian Defense. These were two strong political parties who, like the Nazis in Germany, believed in keeping the ruling class in power. They had an extreme sense of nationalism, which made them hate any ethnic minorities, such as the Jews or the gypsies, who lived in their country.

During most of World War II, Romania's leaders supported Nazi Germany. It was not until 1944, one year before Germany was defeated, that Romania switched to the side of the Allies. Romania's leaders saw that it would be better for them to side with the victors. The Allies were the United States, Great Britain, France and the Soviet Union.

Soviet troops marched into Romania in 1944 and continued to occupy the country after the war ended. The Soviets took control of Romania politically. They set up a Communist form of government.

Communism is a political and economic system in which all property is owned by the state. It is based on the idea that all people should share equally in the wealth of a nation. Businesses and property should be owned in common by the people. That way, Communists believe, there will be no

Romanian citizens celebrate as Soviet tanks enter Bucharest during World War II.

upper and lower classes, no rich and poor.

But in reality, the Communists in Romania simply exchanged one form of dictatorship for another. The dictatorship of the "right" was exchanged for the dictatorship of the "left."

Soviet Plans

The Soviets made Romania a "satellite" of their empire. A satellite state is a smaller nation controlled by a larger, more powerful one. Poland, Czechoslovakia and other nations in Eastern Europe all became satellites of the Soviet Union after World War II.

As a satellite, Romania could supply the Soviets with products at much cheaper prices than other trading partners. In return, Romania would get leadership and military defense from the Soviets.

Romania became very different as a Soviet satellite. Its new constitution was modeled after the Soviets'. Its educational, military and legal systems followed the Soviet models too. Even the names of streets in Romania's big cities became Russian ones!

Changes in the Economy

Before the Communist victory Romania's economy was based on agriculture. More than 80 percent of the people worked as farmers. Much of the land was held by the wealthy few. But there were many small farms owned by peasants too.

However, this system changed in the late 1940s and 1950s. The land was taken over by the government. No one was allowed to own his own farm. Instead, many farms were merged into a few gigantic *kolkhozes,* or collective farms. The farmers rented the land they once owned from the government. And the government decided what crops should be grown.

Industry also changed greatly when communism came to Romania. There had not been many factories before. However, the big, new collective farms could be run effectively with a smaller work force. This freed many people to move to the cities and work in new plants and factories. Oil refineries, chemical plants and automobile factories sprang up in the cities. Mining became even more important, as fuel was needed to keep the new factories going.

"What about Romania?"

Many Romanians were not happy with the changes the Soviets made. They did not want their country to be a mere satellite of the Soviet Union. For one thing, they felt the trading arrangement with the Soviets was very one-sided. Romania had to agree to sell goods to the Soviet Union at very low prices. However, when Romania needed to buy products from the Soviets, prices were very high. None of this seemed fair.

Gheorghe Gheorghiu-Dej, the premier of Romania, went along with this for a little while. Historians say he was afraid to anger the powerful leader of the Soviet Union, Joseph Stalin.

However, after Stalin died in 1953 Gheorghiu-Dej spoke out. He challenged the strict authority the Soviets had over Romania. Then, in 1964, Romania issued an important statement. It said that Romania wanted to be Romania, not just a satellite.

Romania declared its right to choose its own trading partners. Its leaders were also free to decide foreign policy. No longer would Romania be merely a copy of the Soviet Union. Romanian leaders were quick to point out that they did not wish to stop being Communist or to stop being part of the Soviet Union's group of Communist nations. They were not strong enough to throw off Soviet influence completely.

Over the next several years Romania formed new trade agreements. Some of these agreements were with Western nations, such as the United States and France. Some were with Communist countries outside the Soviet orbit, such as China.

A New Leader

Premier Gheorghiu-Dej died in 1965. He had fought hard to build a strict Communist government, but at the same time he tried to create an independent nation for the people of Romania. His successor was Nicolae Ceausescu.

Gheorghe Gheorghiu-Dej, the Romanian Communist leader who helped his country win partial independence from Soviet rule in 1964

ROMANIA UNDER CEAUSESCU

Nicolae Ceausescu was a Communist who had many of the same beliefs as Premier Gheorghiu-Dej. The transition between the two leaders was a very smooth one.

A Favorable Impression

Like Gheorghiu-Dej, Ceausescu believed in a strong, independent Romania. He wanted to remain part of the group of Communist nations in Europe, called the Warsaw Pact nations. But he did not want the Soviets to tell him what nations he could trade with or what nations he could be friendly with.

The most courageous act of Ceausescu's regime occurred in 1968. It was then that the Soviet Union sent in troops to put down a rebellion in Czechoslovakia. The Soviets expected other Warsaw Pact nations to help by sending troops too. However, Ceausescu refused. Polish and Hungarian leaders condemned him for being disloyal to the Soviet Union. Western leaders—including U.S. President Richard Nixon— applauded Ceausescu's independence and spunk.

A Changed Man

But there was much below the surface in Ceausescu's Romania. Some historians believe that he grew more hungry for power and wealth as time went on.

One reporter who spent years studying Romania believes that Ceausescu changed when he visited Asian nations. In some of the nations of the Far East, there has always been a belief in something called the "mandate from heaven." It means, simply, that an emperor's power comes from God. No one except God, according to this belief, can limit or end such a mandate. According to reports, Ceausescu was very impressed by the idea of a mandate from heaven.

He combined a desire for more power and fame with the ideas of communism. As the years went on, he became a dictator—one who made every decision for Romania and who had to answer to no one.

Pig Snouts and Chicken Feet

In its many dealings with other countries, Romania had built up a large debt. Foreign nations had lent money for building schools and roads. Some nations had helped by getting factories started. But all of this money had to be repaid.

Ceausescu did not want to owe money to other nations. Owing money made Romania dependent, and he never wanted to be dependent. So he began a program aimed at repaying the $21 billion debt.

Ceausescu came up with the money by punishing his people. He sold many of the things his country needed.

Romania, a nation with some of the richest soil in Europe, was suddenly without food. On orders from Ceausescu,

Because Ceausescu sold most of the food grown in Romania to other countries, there were often shortages, and people had to stand in long lines to buy basic supplies like milk and eggs.

most of the nation's food was sold to other countries. Money from this went to repay the debt.

Ceausescu's plans called for rationing, or limiting, all of the basic foods his people needed. Meat, milk and cheese were very rare. "Butter?" scoffed one Romanian woman. "I know only one thing about butter—how to spell it! Ask me what I could find in the stores and I'll tell you—pig snouts and chicken feet. That's garbage!"

Almost everything that could be eaten or drunk was in short supply. One writer reported that at Romanian bars there was no beer or wine, so the men sat around eating watermelon!

Shivering through the Winter

In addition to rationing food, Ceausescu cut down on the amount of fuel people could use. Most of the country's heating oil and electricity were sold to other nations. That left Romanians with cold homes and poorly lighted, dark streets.

"Our family forgot what it was like to be warm last winter," says a teacher from Bucharest. "There was no heat, and we all wore layers of clothes plus topcoats—even to bed. The electricity was shut off except for three hours each day. Even so, you couldn't read by the dim light."

Keeping Romania Young

It was important to Ceausescu that Romania's population grow. He wanted a large work force and a large army. For these things the population must be young.

To urge families to have more children, Ceausescu made birth control and abortion illegal. All women were told that they must have at least five children. Those who didn't were forced to undergo medical tests. The tests would show whether those women were using illegal birth control methods.

The plan was despised by Romanians. With food so scarce, many women did not have the strength to bear children. They could barely care for the ones they already had. Many babies died because their homes were too cold or because they did not get enough to eat. Tens of thousands were left in orphanages. Their parents simply could not handle another mouth to feed.

"I'd Burn It to the Ground"

Another of Ceausescu's goals was to modernize the nation. Despite the changes the Communists brought after World War II, Romania has remained a rural country, with

Ceausescu wanted to increase the population of Romania, so he forced families to have many children. A lot of these children ended up in orphanages when their parents could not afford to raise them.

most of its people living on farms. Although the farms have been collective since the Communists took over, each farm family has always had a small cottage. Next to the cottages were small plots of land on which the families grew their own supplies of fruits and vegetables.

But Ceausescu believed that such a system was not efficient. Precious farmland that could be used to grow food was being wasted on private gardens. Beginning in 1986, he told his people, a new plan of modernization would take place.

According to the plan, half of Romania's 15,000 villages would be bulldozed to the ground. People were given two weeks in which to pack up their belongings. In some cases the government agreed to pay for the value of the cottages, although the payment was less than 20 percent of what the property was worth.

More than one million farmers were affected by this new plan. Each family was assigned a place in what was called an "agro-industrial complex." These were high-rise apartment buildings near the large state farms.

Privacy is lacking in the complexes. Several families share one bathroom and one small kitchen. The walls are extremely thin. Most of the apartments have exposed wiring and plumbing.

Marin Svobodny is sad and angry about the change he and his wife have had to go through. "I built that cottage with my bare hands the year we were married," he says sadly. "My wife and I raised six children there. But now, to exist in a little stall not fit for an animal? It makes me ashamed. If I could, I'd burn it to the ground."

Destroying the Past

Farmers were not the only Romanians to lose their homes under Ceausescu. The dictator also wanted to change the face of the capital city, Bucharest. He thought too much in the city was old. There was too much left over from the centuries before communism.

He decided to spend billions of dollars on large, new buildings. There would be a new government center, called the Palace of the Republic. The plaza in front would have room for an audience of 500,000. Although Romanians are not exactly sure where the money came from, it is believed that much of it came from the sale of the nation's food and fuel.

More than 40,000 people were evicted from their homes to make way for the remodeling. Hundreds of old buildings were razed. Some were churches dating back to medieval times. Many of Ceausescu's new building projects were not finished. Because of the revolution in December 1989, no one knows if they ever will be.

Spending Romania's Money

Ceausescu spent a great deal of money honoring communism in Romania—and honoring himself. Most of this money, according to those who worked with him, was taken from the country illegally. And since Ceausescu's execution, Romanians have heard about the lavish ways in which he spent their money.

His 40-room palace was crammed with expensive paintings and sculptures. Most of these had been taken from Romania's churches and museums. Oriental rugs worth thousands of dollars hung on the walls. Bathroom fixtures were made of gold. So were all the knives, forks and spoons.

While Romanians were starving, the Ceausescus were feeding imported veal and beef to their dog.

The Hero, the Genius

For Ceausescu to remain in power, he tried to appear almost superhuman. He worked hard at this. He urged Romanians to refer to him as "Hero" or "Genius." He made certain that there were large portraits of him and his wife in all public buildings.

By law every bookstore had to have one large section devoted to Ceausescu's 28-volume set of speeches. Artists and writers were urged to create works praising him and his accomplishments. At special Communist party gatherings,

The interior of a room in the Palace of the Republic. Ceausescu ordered many homes and historic buildings destroyed to make room for this building. It has stood unfinished since his death.

A soldier reads a magazine in the bedroom of Ceausescu's mansion after the downfall of the former leader. The lavish home contained many luxuries unavailable to Romanian citizens.

Romanians were required to stand and shout: "Ceausescu—Romania, our pride and esteem."

However, like any dictator, Ceausescu was in a fragile position. He knew that he was greatly outnumbered. He was one man holding power over 23 million.

For that reason, he was constantly worried about people plotting against him. He ordered that all typewriters and computers be registered with the government. That way, he knew what people were able to distribute anti-government material. He tried to control every aspect of the people's lives in order to keep himself in power.

The Dreaded Securitate

Ceausescu remained in power for 24 years. It seems hard to believe that a man as hated as he was could have survived that long. The main reason for his power, say experts, was his security force—the Securitate.

The Securitate was Ceausescu's personal military force. Its members continued to kill Romanian civilians in December 1989 even after the army had turned against the dictator. They were fiercely loyal to Ceausescu, and he had treated them well. While regular soldiers were expected to help out building roads and repairing bridges, the Securitate enjoyed free time. Its members were well trained and armed with more powerful weapons than the army had.

Most of the men of the Securitate were recruited from orphanages. They were brought up to think of the dictator as "the only family they would ever have." It was he who gave them a feeling of trust and kindness.

Securitate members repaid that trust and kindness. To make sure Ceausescu was in no danger of losing his power, they spied on Romanians. Anyone who was suspected of being a rebel had his mail opened and telephone tapped. Securitate agents kept files of handwriting samples belonging to suspected rebels. This way, the agents would know if a Romanian citizen was receiving mail from those people.

Those who were found to be rebels were seized and tortured. Special Securitate agents, called Service K, used whatever means possible to get the names of other rebels. After the December revolution, secret torture rooms used by the Securitate were found.

The Last Straw

It seemed that the last straw for the Romanian people was an event that occurred in the city of Timisoara. Ceausescu had decided in the late 1980s to try to make the Romanian people as much alike as possible. However, there were some ethnic minorities—Germans and Hungarians—who were proud of their heritage. They did not want to forget their culture or their language.

Laszlo Tokes, a Hungarian clergyman from Timisoara, had long spoken out against Ceausescu's policy of "alike-

One of the secret tunnels used by the dreaded Securitate, Ceausescu's secret police, to spy on Romanian citizens

ness." Most of the members of his church were Hungarians. They did not want to turn their backs on their heritage.

But the government disapproved of Tokes's comments and threatened him. His church was ransacked. His family was cut off from rationing books, electricity and water. The people of Timisoara, however, had had enough. Knowing the Securitate would be back to harass Tokes, people formed a ring around his church. They wanted to show that they too believed that the government was wrong. They sang Hungarian songs and burned pictures of Ceausescu. They overturned shelves of Ceausescu's books in stores.

A Horrible Massacre

The number of demonstrators grew into the thousands. The Securitate opened fire with machine guns. As the crowds chanted "Freedom," hundreds of people fell to the ground, dead or injured. Many were children, for the young were in the first few rows of protesters.

The next day Ceausescu ordered helicopters and tanks to be sent in. People were dying by the thousands, according to witnesses. When there were no more protesters left, the Securitate forces went door to door. Throughout the village, they shot anyone with a Hungarian-sounding name. Estimates of the dead range from 3,000 to 6,000 people.

As news of the massacre at Timisoara spread, Romanians grew more and more angry. "We realized that what

Laszlo Tokes, the Hungarian clergyman who spoke out against Ceausescu's policies. Thousands of people were massacred by Securitate soldiers when they gathered at Tokes's church to protect him.

happened to those poor devils in Timisoara could have happened to us," said a mechanic from Bucharest. "The people lying in those mass graves, their families digging them up to identify them. Romania is like Nazi Germany now, and that's a shame."

A few days later, when Ceausescu spoke to the Romanian people in Bucharest, those feelings came pouring out as catcalls and boos.

OUT OF THE SHADOWS

Romania did not solve its problems merely by executing Ceausescu. Problems caused by the dictator's policies continue to this day.

Some Quick Solutions

After the overthrow and execution of Ceausescu, the National Salvation Front (NSF) declared itself the new government. Its leader, Ion Iliescu, had been a high-ranking Communist under Ceausescu. However, Iliescu assured Romanians that he was not at all like their dead dictator. He promised to be fair, and as soon as the situation became stable, elections would be held.

Iliescu and his NSF party quickly tried to solve some of Romania's problems. Birth control and abortion were made legal, and thousands of women lined up to take advantage of the changes in the law. Food shelves were suddenly stacked with meat, bread, milk and other hard-to-get items.

Who's Really Elected?

Iliescu's NSF party made many Romanians happy. Workers who had been scraping by on very low wages suddenly found their paychecks larger. There was a general feeling of relief in the air, as if a great weight had been lifted.

However, many Romanians were suspicious, and remain so. After Iliescu won the national election in May 1990, many worried about a former Communist taking over the leadership.

"What difference does it make that he calls himself a National Salvation Front candidate?" asked one college student. "Iliescu is a Communist through and through. He was Gorbachev's friend in college, after all. To pretend he's something else is foolishness."

The election also resulted in many hard feelings. There were accusations that the voting was rigged and that many people were threatened that they must vote for the NSF. Thousands of Romanians protested the NSF's leadership in Bucharest. They camped out in the city square and held rallies. Some began hunger strikes, vowing not to eat until the Communists gave up power.

Thousands of angry Romanians gathered in January 1990 to voice their disapproval of the National Salvation Front, the group that came to power after Ceausescu's execution. The protesters demanded an end to communism in Romania.

Bringing in the Miners

In June the newly elected Iliescu became angry at the protesters. They were calling for him to resign and to have new elections.

To chase the protesters from the square, Iliescu called on miners from the north. Thousands of miners, armed with clubs and heavy hammers, marched into Bucharest. The army also was ordered to shoot protesters who became too unruly. Violence, death and injury resulted from the battles between miners and demonstrators.

So Much to Do

Even if leadership issues are worked out, Romania still has many problems. Health care is at an all-time low. Thousands of people are dying of AIDS—especially young children. The reason for this is that syringes are being reused in hospitals. The fatal disease is spread by dirty needles from one patient to another.

Romania's orphanages are overflowing. Thousands of infants and toddlers wait to be adopted or claimed by their parents. One Western doctor who visited such an orphanage told a sad story:

"The tiny ones stand in their cribs all day long," she said. "They hold their arms out, hoping someone will pick them up. They long for human touch, but no one has the time, for

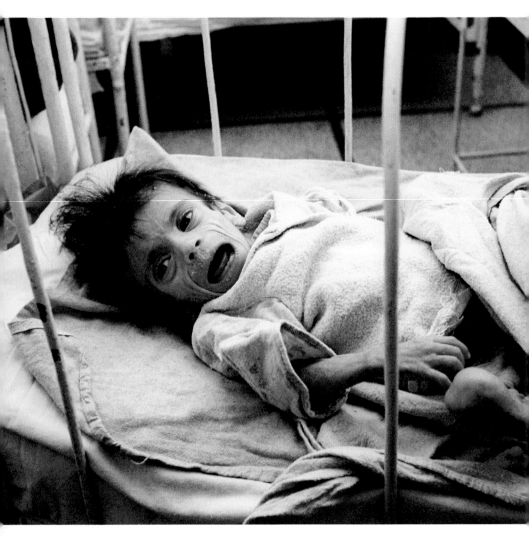

A baby with AIDS. The fatal disease is a great health concern in Romania, where shortages of medical supplies mean that infected syringes are often used several times.

there are so many that are ill. There are no toys or windows. These are the saddest places on earth."

There are some orphanages in Romania today that are more than sad. These are the places where the government has put thousands of children who seem to be handicapped or ill. Here the children are cruelly treated and allowed to starve to death. Toys sent to them by outsiders are left unopened because the children would, in the words of one orphanage worker, "only ruin them."

These particularly terrible institutions have only recently become known to Western reporters. They compare them to the German concentration camps of World War II. But the reporters also point out that the Romanian people themselves allow the institutions to exist—even after the downfall of Ceausescu.

The Dirtiest Air in the World

During the Ceausescu years there was great pressure for factories to increase production. In most Western nations factories have certain rules they must follow to limit the amount of pollution they give off. But in Romania there are no such standards. Besides, many of the factories are outdated. They pump tons of soot and smoke into the air every day. In Romania the environment has been ignored for many years.

One magazine reporter went to a little town in Romania called Copsa Mica. That town's main industry is tire production. The factories run 24 hours a day. The air is so thick with smoke that the reporter said he could taste it.

The pictures he took of the people show dirty, soot-stained faces. Most of the children have lung and eye infections. Everyone coughs—painful, racking coughs.

The grass is inky black, and many of the trees are too poisoned to grow leaves. Farmers say that horses in Copsa Mica die within a year, for their lungs simply give out.

Nowhere to Go but Up

"Romania is the most unfortunate place on earth," said one visitor. Many would agree. There are so many problems that it would be easy for the people simply to give up.

However, many Romanians know that they must fight for their future. They must band together to get a government that will represent them all.

"Most important of all," says a teacher from Timisoara, "is that whatever we do, we do it soon."

Workers in Copsa Mica. Tire manufacturing plants in this town produce a thick black soot that covers everything. Many people suffer from eye and lung diseases.

FACTS ABOUT ROMANIA

Capital: Bucharest

Population: 23,800,000

Official language: Romanian

Chief products:
   Agricultural: corn, fruits, potatoes, sheep, wheat
   Manufacturing: clothing, food, iron ore, machinery,
      natural gas, petroleum and petroleum products

Glossary

communism *A political system based on the idea that all people in a country should share wealth equally. In a Communist country all businesses and property are owned by the state.*

conservative *A person who is slow to change.*

dictator *A leader who holds total control of a country's government.*

Fascist *A person who believes that one's nationality and race are more important than individual liberty. A Fascist supports a strong, dictatorial form of government.*

kolkhoz *A large collective farm. Under the Communist system, many farms are combined to make one large one.*

"left" *A political term applied to people who desire change in the name of greater freedom for the individual.*

Nazi *A member of the National Socialist party that ruled Germany from 1933 to 1945 under Adolf Hitler.*

peasant *A poor farmer.*

"right" *A political term applied to people who oppose change and believe in a government that strongly controls the people.*

satellite *A small nation controlled by a larger one.*

Securitate *The secret police of Romania who protected Ceausescu.*

Index